Seven

Joy's Comprehensive Story To Loving Thy Neighbor

Krystal Akins

Copyright © 2023 Krystal Akins
All rights reserved.
ISBN 9798864117255
Printed in the United States of America

I dedicate this book to the youth.

Forgive.

Release.

Conquer.

Receive.

"If ye fulfill the royal law according to the scripture, Thou shalt love thy neighbour as thyself, ye do well." - James 2:8 (KJV)

Table of Contents

Introduction 5
Chapter 1 13
Chapter 2 17
Chapter 3 25
Chapter 4 29
Chapter 5 38
Chapter 6 42
Chapter 7 46
Chapter 8 50
Chapter 9 58
Chapter 10 64
Chapter 11 70
Chapter 12 75
Chapter 13 80
Chapter 14 84
Chapter 15 94
Chapter 16 98
Chapter 17 106
Chapter 18 111

Chapter 19 115

Chapter 20 119

Chapter 21 124

Chapter 22 128

Chapter 23 132

Chapter 24 138

Chapter 25 144

Chapter 26 150

Chapter 27 154

Chapter 28 157

Chapter 29 160

Chapter 30 163

Introduction

"Who shall ascend into the hill of the Lord? Or who shall stand in his holy place? He that hath clean hands; and a pure heart; who has not lifted up his soul unto vanity, nor sworn deceitfully." –
Psalms 24:3–4 (KJV)

"**Joy!**" In the depths of my sleep, a piercing voice shattered the tranquility. It was a voice I recognized, yet it felt distant and distorted. It was my mom, urgently summoning me to leave my cozy bed. Exhausted from staying up all night watching videos until the early hours of the morning, I felt an overwhelming fatigue that made it nearly impossible to rise on this Saturday morning—a day reserved for cleaning. I knew I was in for a world of trouble if I didn't touch the floor before my mom came up the stairs to my bedroom. My body, however, refused to cooperate. Despite my efforts to get up, dizziness forced me to lay back down. Maybe she wouldn't come up here, I thought. Yeah, maybe. I foolishly closed my eyes, hoping to buy a few more moments of rest. But before I could comprehend what was happening, my bedroom door swung open.

What began as a few scattered droplets quickly turned into a storm of spit raining down on my arms and face. It was my furious mother, swiftly maneuvering herself around, ensuring she dominated every corner of my vision. Sometimes she would tower over my face, pointing her finger down at me. Other times, she would stoop down, locking eyes with me directly, or lean in close to the side of my face, her eyes shooting daggers in whichever direction she hovered over. Any attempt to shift my body only heightened her anger, leading to an explosive outburst. I had to endure, to keep this confrontation as simple as possible.

Sometimes, when my mom felt disrespected or disappointed, she would remain silent, only to reprimand me later through phone calls with various friends and family members. But today, she unleashed her fury, criticizing me for not appreciating her and my father, for failing to acknowledge all they had done for me. She reprimanded me for my laziness, ordering me to get up immediately.

Using her pointer finger, she pressed it repeatedly into my collarbone, each touch escorted by her relentless yelling. "Joy, I can't believe the state of this room! You must think I'm someone else! Pick up these games, bring your laundry downstairs before it doesn't get washed, and make your bed. You know what?! You've got fifteen minutes before I come back and teach you a lesson, girl! Do you hear me?"

"Yes, Ma'am, I hear you," I responded, my voice compliant.

"You think you can keep disrespecting me and this house?" she continued.

"No, Ma'am," I replied, my words fearful.

"Do you believe you can leave your room in such a mess?"

"No, Ma'am", my words quiet.

"Then start cleaning!"

"Yes, Ma'am."

She began to walk away, a grin forming on her face. "Fourteen fifty-nine, fourteen fifty-eight..."

Glancing at the clock, I realized the countdown had begun. Suddenly, my legs felt weak, as if they were ocean waves threatening to crash to the ground. I managed to regain my balance, quickly standing up. As I did, a silence fell upon us, the calm before a treacherous storm. I looked up at my mother, who no longer yelled but stood in the doorway of my bedroom, breathing heavily. Her stare emotionally burned into me, capable of burning a hole through the new carpet beneath me. I could feel the intensity of her anger and disgust coming from her. It felt as if the air was being sucked out of my body at an alarming rate, and I desperately tried not to inhale any of her toxic energy. In that moment, I resented her, refusing to accept anything she had to offer, including the air she breathed. Amidst my overthinking, guilt washed over me. As she would huff, I would try my hardest not to suck up any of her air. I didn't like her right now and I didn't want to accept any of her including her used air. With my overthinking I felt guilty. I had this weird feeling pass over my soul like a premonition. It was awkward, that feeling, strange- familiar and not familiar at all.

You're sleeping. Echoed my thoughts. *"I am?"* It was so hard to tell. The feeling got stronger, and with every breath it gobbled up my control. It was like sadness or disappointment. Why was this feeling lingering in my thoughts?

My mother's actions suddenly pulled me out of my head, she pulled a belt over her shoulder. I didn't even hear her come into my bedroom. Well, my intuition did. I guess that's what sparked the dream. I felt my eyes widen with fear as she jerked the heavy blanket off me. I almost threw up as she started striking me constantly.

"Are you ignoring me on purpose?!"

"No, Ma'am"

"Do you think you're grown?!"

"No."

"I guess you plan on being useless all your life?!"

As she whupped me, my thoughts took over again, and everything began to happen in slow motion. Thoughts of regret and anger welcomed me. "Why didn't I get up?" "Not only that, why did I act so stupid, and believe myself?" You're dreaming, echoed the voice again. "Oh, yeah," I whispered. "Wake up, wake up, wake up."

BEEP, BEEP, BEEP, screams the alarm clock. I slowly sit on the side of the bed with a stinging headache. I'm in a room concealed in darkness and while it was a part of my new home, it didn't quite feel like my own. Reflecting on the unsettling dream, a surge of anger coursed through my muscles, intensifying the stinging, throbbing pain in my head.

Chapter 1

"Beloved, let us love one another: for love is of God; and everyone that loveth is born of God, and knoweth God. He that loveth not knoweth not God; for God is love." (1 John 4:7-8, KJV)

Placing my left hand over my heart, I took slow, deliberate breaths, attempting to calm myself down. But no matter how hard I tried, my heartbeat only quickened, thumping like a relentless drum. In that moment, it felt like all the memories of my mother were slipping away, leaving behind only the darkest ones. The beatings, the insults, the overwhelming shame—they consumed my thoughts. My mother's voice echoed in my mind, but her face remained a blur. What was happening to me?

I rose from my bed, silencing the blaring alarm on my cell phone. School awaited, and I couldn't dwell on these questions any longer. It was time to get ready. Restlessly, I paced the bathroom floor adjacent to my room. This small, cramped space was where I lived with Pat—my older brother. His home on Crescent Drive felt like a kingdom he ruled with an iron fist, yet there were moments when he displayed his kindness, taking care of me for the past three years. Pat possessed an air of authority as if he were a god walking among mortals.

Lately, when we argued, he would put up a wall of anger, refusing to address our wounds, leaving us in silence for days. In the past, our fights would drag on for what seemed like an eternity. As a form of punishment, Pat would deny me food or postpone buying essential items like pads, prolonging my suffering. Our relationship now resembled a decaying corpse, slowly deteriorating. He failed me, and I, too, felt like I failed him.

To relax, I immediately told myself the same mantra I repeat every morning before I get dressed and leave. It goes, "Love yourself, Joy. Love yourself as others have loved you. Love yourself as you want to be loved and love yourself as you love your neighbor." I took a deep breath, allowing my heart rate to slow down as I exhaled. No need to panic, I reminded myself, I just needed to refocus my priorities. While brushing my teeth and washing my face, I gently released my curls from my satin bonnet, letting them cascade freely. Thoughts of my father, grandmother, and Kismet, an old teacher's aide who always showed me love and friendship, filled my mind, grounding me in their warmth.

Slipping into my heavy, fur-lined coat and lifting my trusty Jansport backpack onto my shoulders, a sudden realization hit me—I remembered that today was my birthday. How could I have forgotten something so important? Just to be sure, I hurriedly approached the phone, my anticipation mounting. As soon as the screen illuminated, it confirmed my fears: January 24th stared back at me. My heart sank, the weight of disappointment settling in.

Chapter 2

"Finally, be ye all of one mind, having compassion one of another, love as brethren, be pitiful, be courteous."- 1 Peter 3:8

As I walk to the front of the house to leave, I see pink timberlands beside my black timberland snow boots. I'm glad Vena came back after all the terrible stuff she's been through with Pat. Vena's been my brother's girlfriend since middle school and it's been a tough journey for them.

Being sure to be as quiet as I possibly can, I check my jean pocket and make sure I have my bus pass and my last five I had from my allowance from 2 weeks ago. I run my hand through my bag before thrusting all its weight on my right shoulder to feel for my sketchbook, everything's here. I open and close the door slowly. Once outside, I stuck the silver key in the lock and turn it until I hear the door seal with a clunk. Just to be sure, I check the doorknob, it's good. I tuck my key in my shirt after dropping it over my head and place my skullcap on like nothing matters at all. My brother's matte black truck is parked with barely any frost on the windshield. So, Pat hasn't been in long, he must have worked another double shift at the bread factory or stayed out late to win back Vena. As I stand there in the snow, a sense of unease starts to creep in. Without wasting anytime, I break into a jog down the alley, before he has a chance to notice I'm gone.

As I wait at the bus stop, the sounds of two guys rapping, accompanied by the beats of another person, fill the air. A small group gathers, and their oohs and aahs echo around me. The rhythm takes hold of me, and I feel myself being transported away from my own problems. My mind becomes still, just like the frozen Michigan weather that surrounds me.

But my momentary escape is interrupted as the bus pulls up, shifting the snow onto the concrete and drenching my boots. Stepping onto the bus, my mind still lingers on the question: What is love? Yet, my thoughts are suddenly distracted by a younger kid, who is physically smaller than me but blocks my path by extending his foot, fixing his gaze upon me or perhaps right through me. Carefully, I step over his knee, making my way towards the middle of the bus.

As I reach the middle, I notice that there are two seats, yet both girls sitting next to the empty seats by them stretch out their hands, claiming the empty seat beside them. I continue to walk, reaching the back of the bus. Where there is a seat with a black backpack in it. It's squeezed between a girl from my neighborhood that speaks to me from time to time and dresses weird. She is rude and has an attitude to match, but I ask for the seat as the driver yells for me to sit down. The girl looks up at me frustrated, taking her earphones down. "This is for my friend, and if you're still sitting here when she gets on she will put them hands on you."

The bus driver yells again, "Sit down or get off."

The girls shakes her head in carelessness and jerks the bag off the seat.

Love, you know? It's like these thoughts of it keep fluttering around in my head, but I can never quite catch hold of any solid memories or hopes for what it could be in my life. They just float away, like butterflies slipping through my fingers. Anyway, here I am on this old, rickety city bus, rocking back and forth, desperately trying to make it to school by 6:30. The bus stops and starts, picking up more students along the way.

I always opt for the early bus, just like a bunch of other kids. Some of them want to grab an early bite because they didn't

Love Thy Neighbor

have much to eat the night before, while others are trying to avoid certain people who give off predator vibes, you know? But for me, taking the early bus is more about escaping from my fears and shame as soon as possible. Funny thing is, most of us on this bus are failing at life and falling apart at the same time as we rush to be the first ones at school. We're the "first people," or maybe more like the last. It's like a silent inside joke I share with myself.

Out of nowhere, this memory pops up in my head. It's about how I found out about the early buses in the first place, the ones that could take me away from all the chaos. It was on one of those nights at home when Patrick was spewing his toxic anger at Vena and me. The air was heavy with his rage and irritation, making it hard to breathe. So, there I was, sitting in silence, staring at the ceiling, feeling trapped. That's when I noticed her for the first time, the girl I occasionally talked to. She was walking through the alley behind my brother's place before the crack of dawn, at 5:30 in the morning. It caught my attention because I had seen her there before, you know? Sometimes she would be in a hurry, rushing through the alley. Other times she would take slow, deliberate steps. Something about her made me curious. So, without wasting any time, I got up and got dressed really quick. I knew she would pass by the alley again. And there she was, like clockwork. When I reached the stop sign at the end of the road, I couldn't help but ask her, "Hey, why do you always leave so early?"

She looked at me with this blank expression before replying, "Lots of kids wait at the stop early, you know? It's better than being alone in the dark, all curled up and waiting for the sun to rise."

I nodded, getting what she meant.

"You're out here this morning, so you know exactly what I'm talking about," she said, her tone cold.

Love Thy Neighbor

I was speechless because she was right on the money.

We both sat there in silence, waiting for the first bus to show up. Our breaths mingled in the faint darkness, almost like we were chain smokers or something. With that the memory faded.

Finally, the bus arrived, reaching its last stop. I knew her friend would be getting on now. And sure enough, she was the first one to hop on the moment those doors opened. I bet the girl with the headphones had given her a heads-up through a text, because she looked pissed off, pushing her way to the back. Uh-oh, I braced myself as she approached our seat. Fury blazed in her eyes, and her hair was all over the place like she had just rolled out of bed. Suddenly, she grabbed my hair through my hat and snapped, "Move!" I tried to pry her hands off me with one hand while reaching for my pepper spray in my side pocket with the other, but it slipped away from my fingertips, so I couldn't grab it. The headphone girl grabs both my hands tightly as her friend is hitting my face and chest, suddenly she stops. Removing a small blade from under her coat sleeve. Seeing it the bus driver yells loudly "stop, put the weapon down!"

Chapter 3

"Be ye angry, and sin not: let not the sun go down upon your wrath: Neither give place to the devil."- Ephesians 4:26-27

So, there we were, both yanked off the bus by the security guards upon arrival. The coffee-brown, slender old bus driver stuck his head out of the doors and yelled, "You two stay off this bus since you can't follow the rules!" And with that, he drove off, leaving us standing there as the last few students trickled out. I could feel their eyes on us, judging and scrutinizing, just like my mother's eyes from this morning. But they're wrong, just like she is. They don't know the whole story.

The security guards escorted us to the office, where we were directed to these uncomfortable, tattered blue seats. We had to wait for the principal, Mr. Carliyal, to show up. Now, let me tell you, Mr. Carliyal is a peculiar character. He's super organized, but he always seems so uneasy around us, like he can't quite figure us out. When he's upset, he starts fidgeting and stuttering. And you know what's even weirder? He often purses his lips so tightly together before speaking that it looks like he is not even breathing. He's this stout Mexican man with dark skin and slicked-down hair. Before he even gets a proper "good morning" from his receptionist and a sip of his strong coffee, she nods in our direction, not even bothering to make eye contact, to let him know we're here.

Mr. Carliyal motions for us to come into his office, and he immediately sits down at his computer and starts clicking away. "Ladies," he begins, without giving us a chance to speak, "there must be some deeply troubling issues at home if you're waking up angry and beating me to my office." The girl and I try to explain ourselves, but he cuts us off, not interested in hearing our side of the story. "From now on, you both need to catch the 7 o'clock bus to arrive at school by 7:45. And as for the consequences, you're suspended for three days. So, I'll see you ladies on Tuesday. Make sure you arrange for a ride to pick you up."

He then turns to the spider-like receptionist, who's juggling telephones and signing late passes at lightning speed, and instructs her to add us to her workload. Now she's responsible for the two of us. Mr. Carliyal sternly tells her not to let us leave until she hands over the suspension slip to whoever comes to pick us up. With that, he abruptly gets up from his chair, slams the door shut behind us, and disappears.

As we stand in the hallway, we can hear the sounds of chaos coming from Mr. Carliyal's office. It's like a symphony of loud, fearful sprays, chairs moving, and a window squeaking open. It's all happening behind that closed door, and we can't help but wonder what on earth is going on in there. He really is strange.

Chapter 4

"As one whom his mother comforteth, so will I comfort you; and ye shall be comforted in Jerusalem." - Isaiah 66:13 (KJV)

Both of us step out of the office, as quiet as mice. Passion takes out her bulky phone and attempts to call her mom using three different numbers. The first call Passion made I overhear the disconnected message, followed by a message telling her to dial another number. The second call connects her to a dismissive older woman who says something cruel. All I catch before she slams the phone down in anger is a frustrated "huh, GG, have you seen my mom?" A man answers the last call, and I can hear her mom's voice in the background. She asks to speak to Cynthy, and after a brief exchange, the man hangs up. Looking at her tired face, I can see the exhaustion etched in her toffee-colored eyes. They seem dimmed by heavy eyelids. There is so much I can read on her face, it overwhelms my mind thinking what maybe a few is now amplified to millions, and maybe she can see the same million things on mine.

When Passion got onto the bus in a rush, her hair was hidden under a hood. But as she scratched her head repeatedly, the hood fell back, revealing a head full of bright yellow curls. Each curl seemed distinct and vibrant. Her face appeared downcast, as if it were being pulled toward the floor. Her lips, adorned with shimmering light pink smeared lip gloss, both lips were full like Ziploc bags of heavy potato salad. She seemed so solemn and being near her made me feel depressed. Breathing became a struggle, as my chest tightened, and my throat felt constricted.

Whenever that deep sadness creeps into my heart, I instinctively grab my sketchbook and create in my comic strip world. I reach into my bag and pull it out, seeking solace in drawing. I tap on the cover debating myself, should I?

Love Thy Neighbor

"Ay yo what is that?" Passion asked.

"Oh I sketch…well draw." I said without even lifting my eyes from the cover.

"Draw, ain't that for little kids?" Passion sounded irritated.

"No, it helps me to relax. What do you do to relax since you're on me?" I asked.

Passion paused "relax, man whatever."

She turned her head as the receptionist loudly screeched "Shhh!"

I slowly flip the cover back and push past the thick paper. Lost in my own thoughts, I sketch my recurring heroine, Seven. She wields a massive sword, scraping it against the cold concrete, almost sparking a flame. The words "love thy neighbor" adorn the blade. Seven feels so real to me, and I allow her to come alive on the pages with the ink flowing from my pen.

After what feels like an hour, the office door finally opens. I snap out of my melodic dance with Seven. A woman, no taller than the gloomy stranger, enters. She's wearing pink slippers, pajama pants, a black tube top, a dinghy fur coat, and black skullcap with metallic-rimmed glasses.

"Uh-uh, get up, Passion! You wanna fight? Get ready, 'cause when you get home, you're gonna have a hell of a fight!" she exclaims.

"Mama," Passion, whines.

"It wasn't my fault. She took my seat on the bus."

"Passion, how the hell can someone take your seat on the bus?" Passion just stares blankly at the ground. The energy in the room shifts, and her mother turns to the woman at the reception desk, snapping her fingers she snips "Um, miss, can I get whatever I need to get out of here?"

As they walk out, I hear Passion's mom scolding her, expressing how much she hates her and her brother for not even being able to go to school and let her work in peace. Passion not only looks tired, but the weight of sadness is evident in her eyes, the same sadness that crawled up my heart like a sickness.

With a heavy heart, I continue sketching, depicting a girl bent over with roots resembling a tree emerging from her calves. My hero, Seven, leaps into the air, ready to sever the roots that once held her captive—roots made of concrete, wood, and the weight of the world. But before the roots could be severed a red dragon swoops around in the sky plotting on the girl. People spill out of the town stores and point at the ferocious dragon. What will Seven do to complete her mission and save the girl? A woman begins to scream frantically calling the girl to free herself as she once had to herself.

"Get up! Save yourself!" She shouted.

The girl looking defeated sadly hung her head a hardened into a tree, slowly calcifying. Seven runs towards the people…

Startled by the air conditioner coming on I forgot that earlier, I pretended to call my brother, hoping to avoid Passion seeing him. I know Pat stayed out late, and he would not be in a cheerful mood to come pick me up. I thought I could figure out another way to leave without involving him. Since my school often overlooked our struggles, where it seemed like nobody knew who had parents, a home, food, or even clothes.

I mustered the courage to approach the receptionist once again. The receptionist, whom I affectionately referred to as the spider in my head, looked up and I motioned for her attention. She nodded solemnly, understanding my request. With my hand feeling like an anchor against my face, I lifted the heavy phone and dialed my brother's number, hoping that his girlfriend Vena would answer and spare me from going through him.

"Hello, Vena," I greeted, my voice hushed.

"Yeah," came her reply.

"I need to be picked up from school. I'm not feeling well. Can you get me instead of Pat?"

In a barely audible whisper, she responded, "Um, I'll ask him to use the truck."

She paused just long enough for me to grasp the weight of my request before saying, "Just be safe and hope it's me walking through the door and not him."

Taking a deep breath, a tear escaped and fell onto the counter. In my mind, I repeated my mantra, seeking solace, urging me to love myself, *love myself as others have loved me, love myself as I wanted to be loved, and love myself as I loved my neighbor.*

Fear clenched me tightly, inflicting pain. Nausea and sickness surrounded me as the office door tormented my senses. People streamed in and out, the constant opening and shutting amplifying my anxiety. I pleaded, wished, and begged God that it would be Vena and not Pat who would arrive. If it were Pat, she would endure his anger most.

Pat, my older brother by four years, was all I had left when our parents tragically died in a flood at a community center three years ago. It happened off Montgomery Blvd. We used to have an older sister, ten years my senior, but she disappeared shortly after what was meant to be a memorial for our parents. Pat's dreams of attending college and playing football for Oklahoma were

Love Thy Neighbor

shattered by their deaths, and he had to stay here in Michigan with me. I really hope he doesn't come to pick me up…

Chapter 5

"Blessed are they that mourn: for they shall be comforted."
Matthew 5:4 (KJV)

Crying isn't something to be ashamed of. It's a natural release, a way to cleanse the soul. Tears should only flow when someone is truly sad, incredibly happy, filled with joy, or even bursting with pride. But somehow, in this world, crying has become so normalized that even when tears grace the faces of our loved ones, they carry no hint of sorrow, no empathy, no pain. How did life become so bleak that everyone I encounter seems incapable of shedding tears, except in fits of anger?

I'm hurting, breaking apart, and I can see that my brother is hurting too. Yet, he channels his pain into a dark abyss, fueling misery and perpetuating a cycle of tyranny. He inflicts his anger on me and even on his loving girlfriend, who has been by our side since long before the accident. Vena, with her wide smile and colorful braces, used to be full of life. She was an athlete, running track and playing golf. I used to be so certain about my passion for swimming, but somehow back then she even sparked my interest in fencing, tennis, and pep rallies. But now, Vena moves slowly, speaks softly, and seems almost devoid of vitality.

Vena remains with us because her love for Pat and me runs deep, I can sense it. Despite her family's concerns about her drastic transformation, she stays committed to us.. I hesitate to burden her with too much because I fear that if she leaves, it would be just the two of us, Pat and me, alone in this world. Perhaps she can bring back the sunlight we so desperately need. Maybe Vena can share her radiant happiness with us. The only problem is, I'm not entirely certain she has enough of it left to give.

Love Thy Neighbor

With that thought lingering in my mind, I grasp my sketchbook and steal a glance out of the small side window, hoping to catch a glimpse of the familiar truck. But before my pencil can even find its rhythm on the coarse sketch paper, the door abruptly clicks and slams shut.

"Hi, badass," a voice greets me, cutting through the heavy silence.

It's Pat.

Chapter 6

"A soft answer turneth away wrath: but grievous words stir up anger." Proverbs 15:1 (KJV)

As we hopped into the truck, which was oddly parked in front of the high school instead of the usual parking lot, Pat looked completely drained and just wanted to head home for some rest.

"So, you got a problem understanding?" Pat grumbled as he slammed the door shut.

"No, it's not a misunderstanding that caused the fight," I replied, my voice steady but tinged with unease.

"No, not the fight I just heard about. You feel sick, huh?" Pat pressed, his voice growing louder.

"Answer me!" he yelled, his anger reverberating through the truck. The tension in the air was suffocating.

Everything seemed to freeze in that moment. The keys dangled from the ignition, swinging back and forth without actually starting the engine. I felt frozen, like I was stuck in quicksand. My heart pounded against my ribs, my throat tightened, and tears welled up in my heavy eyes, streaming down my cheeks silently as I whimpered. Pat's grip on my coat tightened, squeezing my breasts together, and I couldn't help but cry. The truck roared to life as he started it, driving us toward our so-called home. Nervousness coursed through me as Pat continued his tirade.

"Sick for what? 'Cause the only sick person here is me!" he ranted, his words cutting deep. "And you got my girl mixed up in this crap! You're sick, and if I had any sense, I'd dump your sorry ass in juvie or a loony bin and walk away. You know what?!

You're nothing! You're pathetic! A burden, Joy, always making everything about yourself! I can't wait to kick you out and figure out my own life!"

Pat's anger seemed to feed off itself, spiraling out of control. Sadly, I had grown accustomed to this pattern. "She ain't your girl, she's mine!" he spat, shooting me a piercing glare while we idled helplessly at a long red light. Overwhelmed by a wave of emotions, my heart threatened to give up, and darkness closed in as I passed out.

Chapter 7

"*When my heart is overwhelmed: lead me to the rock that is higher than I.*" - Psalm 61:2 (KJV)

When I wake up, I jolt upright in the truck, parked out front in the yard. My heart races as I glance at my phone. An hour has passed since Pat picked me up. I reach for my sketchbook and flip through its worn pages. My eyes widen as I see Seven, her sword slashing across the throat of a mighty dragon. I freeze, astonished by the dragon's defeat. I struggle to remember where I left off with my sketches at school, but it escapes me, lost in the haze of my thoughts.

Shaking off the confusion, I refocus and hastily start sketching. The dragon's head detaches from its body, and Seven moves on, speedily approaching the group of people. With her sword, she cuts through two women and five men, including a woman who bears a striking resemblance to Passion's mom. The woman doesn't perish like the dragon, but crimson trails mark her forearms and thighs. Her emotions erupt, shifting from weeping to crying, until her screams pierce the air. Her tears blend with pools of blood, flooding my heart and spilling over into the next panel of my drawing where Seven destroys the dragon.

The tree who was once a girl seems to be dying. The woman appears fragile in the reflection of the stores, and the people in the crowd try to console her. As the crowd realizes the dragon's threat has ended, they exchange sad and bewildered glances. Without much thought, I instinctively draw a cloud above them, questioning, "What will we do now?"

Rain drops begin and the people run under the leaves of the tree. Softening the girls heart and watering her roots. As the rain slows she's released. A girl again but this time alive with dragon blood, strangers needs, and Seven's courage.

Seven walks away, emanating bravery, confidence, and heroism — a figure of justice in black and white. She sheathes her ancient sword back into its pouch after scraping it against the concrete once more. A triumphant smirk graces her face, masked in black paint over her mouth, as I complete the frame, capturing her fulfilled expression.

Love Thy Neighbor

Chapter 8

"The LORD is my light and my salvation; whom shall I fear? the LORD is the strength of my life; of whom shall I be afraid?" - Psalm 27:1 (KJV)

I stumble out of the truck, catching a glimpse of Vena through the sweltering haze. Minutes after finishing my sketch, her voice pierces through the chaos, calling out to me from the window. I enter the house cautiously, my steps heavy, only to find Vena hovering over my unconscious brother in the living room. My eyes are puffy from crying earlier..

"Vena... what happened to Pat, is he going to be okay? Is he hurt, Is he... dead?" I asked worried.

Vena turned to me; her face filled with worry.

"Joy, I hit Pat with the dog chain and when he wouldn't quit, I smashed the lamp over his head."

"Quit?!" I asked confused.

"Yes, Pat came in and started fighting with me, he pushed me into the refrigerator and told me to make breakfast since we would all be here. While I was grabbing the eggs he started squeezing my shoulder into the fridge with the fridge door. I put my foot in the fridge and the eggs dropped to the ground. Pat was so mad he tried to choke me, but I grabbed the chain off the wall while running into the living room. He grabbed my hair and I started to hit him with the dog chain! He wouldn't stop, Joy! So I grabbed the lamp by the cord on the ground and slid the lamp to me and hit him over the head with it! "He's out cold, but he's still breathing. I called 911, Joy. They said they are on the way, but I'm so scared. What if I've made everything worse?"

"Vena, it's it ok, everything is going to be ok. Calling for help was the right thing to do."

"I just... I didn't know what else to do, Joy. He was getting so violent, and I was scared. I'm so tired of being scared. I never wanted it to come to this." "I love him!" "Me, I do!"

"I understand, Vena. None of us wanted it to come to this. Sometimes it feels like we're trapped. We'll figure this out."

"I hope he'll be okay. What if this makes things worse between us? Joy, I had to do something before…"

It's ok Vena. We've been through so much already."

"No, Joy, I'm pregnant."

"Pregnant?"

"Pat and I chose to abort our baby in middle school, and I swore I would never choose to do that again. I stood up for us, Joy, I am saving our baby this time."

"Vena, I …I didn't know."

" I came back last night because after I told Pat he didn't say anything. I left back to my moms and he kept calling me asking me to come back."

"Vena your a sister to me and I promise you're not alone in this. We have each other."

"Thank you, Joy. That means the world to me right now."

"We're stronger together, Vena. We'll get through this, no matter what."

I can't believe this is happening. Pat has been so angry lately, so full of rage... I don't understand why he's hurting himself and us. I thought things would change once I told him. Joy, I've been trying to help him. I've been trying to understand what he's going through, but it's been so difficult. I love him, but I can't keep living in this constant fear and chaos."

"I know, Vena. I know you love him, and I appreciate everything you've done for the both of us. But it's getting worse, and I'm scared too."

Vena reached out and took my trembling hands.

I nod, tears streaming down my face. "You're right. We can't go on like this. We deserve better, and Pat needs help. I don't want to lose him, but I don't want to lose myself either."

Vena squeezed my hands gently "We'll figure this out together, Joy. I'm here for you every step of the way."

I smiled weakly- "Thank you.

As fear consumes me, I start to panic, and tears started streaming down my face. Vena let my hands go slowly and with my vision blurred we both must have realized she's on the edge too, fragile and bewildered, just like me.

Within moments, the wailing sirens of an approaching ambulance reach my brother's front door. I feel myself fading, as if I'm slowly disappearing. I'm nothing more than background noise, insignificant, invisible. Emotions surge within me like treacherous waters, threatening to drown me in a rising typhoon. With a trembling hand, I push open the heavy wooden door. The paramedics rush past me, their purpose clear, and someone taps me on the shoulder. I feel the door slipping from my sweaty left palm.

And then everything goes black.

When I regain consciousness, I find myself surrounded by police officers asking if I'm alright. It should be comforting, but instead, I feel ashamed. I wonder how much time has passed and glance back, hoping to see Vena where she stood before. But she's gone. I cry out, demanding to know where she is, begging for answers, yet all they do is repeat, "Are you okay?" I'm so consumed by sadness that I want to scream from the depths of my soul, to make them leave this place, but I can't produce a single sound. I'm silenced.

Love Thy Neighbor

Chapter 9

"From the end of the earth will I cry unto thee, when my heart is overwhelmed: lead me to the rock that is higher than I."
Psalm 61:2 (KJV)

I make my way to the hospital on foot, as Vena was taken away in one of the last police cars, leaving my brother's front yard behind. She resembled Passion, and in her reflection, I see myself mirrored. The way Passion appeared in the office at school I must look the same now. That realization sends a violent whirlwind through the core of my mind, bringing back a rush of emotions. They surround me, press in on me, filling every inch of my being. I'm being swallowed by sorrow, succumbing to the weight of my loneliness, desperate for connection. Now, I'm overwhelmed by tragedy, sinking deeper into it's the abyss, consumed by swirling thoughts. Pat, my birthday, the fights, the discord, the hatred, the cruelty, the agonizing neglect... the baby. I need my notepad.

I begin to frantically search my bag and here it is under the loose-leaf papers. I sit near a bus stop to use the light as I begin to place the sword in Seven's hand. She runs into a crowd of professionals slicing their arms and tearing through hearts with her brutal passes. She screams for them to move back! To move away! She silences anyone screaming back with any form of authority or disrespect.

As she reaches the back of the crowd, Seven realizes there are thin strings attached to their backs extending upwards towards a towering skyscraper that seemed to pierce the clouds. Seven doesn't even hesitate as she storms up the side of the building crashing into a huge glass plated window and running to the emergency staircase.

As she arrives at the top of the high rise Seven disappears. A huge head falls out what's like the floorboards of heaven. The colossal head was ugly and grey as it cracked the sidewalks where the people once gathered. The head of a giant. A once giant. A hidden giant. A giant no more.

She swoops to the ground and cuts the professionals free. But their scars are still bleeding. As I sweep my lead one last stroke a tear betrays me and falls on the black and white page. Until the next time, Seven.

I gaze up and notice that the once golden-colored sky has turned into a blanket of pitch-black darkness. Determined, I continue walking for another seven blocks until I reach the entrance of Miracle Memorial Hospital. It's as if the place is illuminated with a shining bat symbol, or like New York's Statue of Liberty standing tall in all its nostalgic glory.

Love Thy Neighbor

This is the very hospital where our mother dedicated countless hours, tirelessly tending to patients, following strict orders, working herself to the bone to generate income from the suffering and anguish of others. She saved lives with her boundless compassion, only to eventually meet her own demise alongside my father after the tragic incident.

Love Thy Neighbor

Chapter 10

"But if any provide not for his own, and specially for those of his own house, he hath denied the faith, and is worse than an infidel."

- 1 Timothy 5:8 (KJV)

I'm reluctant to walk the last couple blocks to begin my quest to break into the entrance because I'm scared and fuming inside. I love my brother very much and I genuinely care for Vena. But their fights have never gotten this intense before.

In our emotionally drained home, it's not uncommon for my brother to exert his dominance over Vena, reducing her to silent tears in some forgotten corner. And when he's had one too many drinks, he crashes onto the recliner, only to provoke me with senseless arguments, seeking to get himself riled up and fight with me.

There was this one time when I made the grave mistake of defending Vena. Pat was aware that the hospital would only provide pain medication for broken ribs, thanks to his friend's football injuries back in highschool, my brother resorted to violence. His punches landed forcefully on my side; the impact was so severe that it cracked one of my ribs.

With his smooth talk and quick thinking, he managed to calm Vena down with yet another empty promise. Then, without a care, he chucked a bottle of Tylenol at me, telling me to take the whole thing and shut up, that was about two summers ago.

Telling us both his opinion on sitting in a boring ER overnight sitting there would make him tired. Vena stood up to walk away out of frustration, but Pat quickly got up, stood in her way and forcefully smashed her head into the wall mirror. Blood trickled down onto the brown carpet, staining it. Then he attached the dog collar that belonged to his old dog to her neck, dragging her to the recliner calling her mean names. Once he sat down in the chair, he casually watched a sports newscast on TV, quiet and unfazed by all the grief he caused us. I watched Vena from the dark corner of the living room until she passed out from hyperventilating. I don't believe we ever cleaned the blood from the carpet.

Thinking about that old memory of the "New" Pat hits me hard. And now there's news of a baby? Man, we've already taken so much from him, I didn't think we had anything left in the tank. The upcoming 18th birthday feels like a lifeline, but I can't help but worry about how I'm gonna survive on my own next year.

Vena, on the other hand, still holds onto hope that Pat will change. It's crazy, considering how he's been treating her lately. But today, she showed some real guts and fought back. It's like a small victory for love or something. But dang, with this baby news thrown into the mix, things just got even more complicated. It's a wild mix of emotions—hope, uncertainty, and a bit of fear about what's to come.

I think they found a way to live, I mean nothing fazes Vena anymore when Pat does something to her. No tears, no outbursts, just this numbness and passive fear. It's like her fighting spirit has dried up, and I can't help but wonder how she found the strength to fight back today after being so beaten down for years.

The thought of my brother possibly being seriously hurt is suffocating. What if he goes to jail? And now he's going to be a dad, I'm speechless.

But the idea of losing everyone who has been my anchor, my sense of safety and belonging, threatens to break me. I don't think I'll survive losing another family member. It would be a death of my own, not just mentally or emotionally, but in every fiber of my being.

I'm in full belief that all those "sorry for your loss" or "let me know ifs..." have expirations attached to them. All the reach out to me" never seem to answer or even reach back. Death is really isolating. Loss is like a magic trick; people, places, and things you once had security in or access to seem to disappear. No longer do the people in those areas of your life seem to remember you or know how you operate when you lose. A lot more seemed to remember what happened when you happen to show up, they look shocked that you even exist even though you lost someone and weren't the lost person. I started to realize these things early on and began removing myself so I wouldn't have to decipher what anyone else must be thinking.

Love Thy Neighbor

Chapter 11

"Come unto me, all ye that labour and are heavy laden, and I will give you rest." - Matthew 11:28 (KJV)

As I step into the lobby of Miracle Hospital, the hallways and people around me become a labyrinth of confusion. I navigate through, making a left turn effortlessly, and then a few paces later, a right towards the emergency area. But as I walk, a wave of sickness surges through my belly, and I end up heaving what looks like a strawberry milkshake into a nearby fake plant.

When I raise my eyes, I see nurses scurrying about, their sense of urgency palpable. A flickering light catches my attention in the corner of the ceiling, adding to the chaotic atmosphere. Over there, I notice a mother wearing a running hat and jogging pants, holding a baby swaddled in a nursery blanket, hat, and winter coat.

The baby's cries are subdued, yet filled with an unsettling distress, as if he's both tired and in pain.

I feel uneasy, like I care more about that adorable baby more than anyone else in the room. The mom is all focused on filling out paperwork, but she forgot her insurance card and she's begging the clerk to find someone who can help. On the other side of the crowded room there's a solo officer dealing with some scruffy dude who's got holes in his shoes and he's causing a scene, demanding to see his wife who's been in a coma for, like, forever. They're just kicking him out without even checking his story.

I'm a nervous wreck right now. My emotions are all twisted up inside, stretching and aching. And to make matters worse, I haven't eaten a single thing all day, maybe even two days. My stomach is growling like crazy.

On top of that, I took a nasty fall earlier when the ambulance made it to my brother's place now my head and shoulder are killing me. It's like a constant reminder of the pain I'm feeling, both physically and emotionally.

I walk down the hallway notice that my shoes aren't squeaking as much. It's like they're trying to keep things quiet for me. I find a spot between a plant and a chair, and I hunch down, my feet slipping out from under me. I cover my eyes with my hands, feeling that panic welling up inside.

The thought of my brother being seriously hurt, or worse, it's terrifying. I don't want to be left alone in this world. Without him, my life would be empty, full of pain and boredom for years to come. But despite all his anger and sadness, I still love my brother. He stepped up when our parents tragically died in that community center basement. He put his own dreams on hold and became the rock in my life. Without his support, I'd be lost, floating in a sea of uncertainty, bouncing from place to place, or even ending up on the streets. He's my security, my anchor in this crazy world.

But as I'm lost in my thoughts about Pat, I suddenly hear blood hitting the floor and screams echoing through the halls. Police and nursing staff rush past me, swarming around multiple people. It snaps me back to reality, reminding me of the urgency of my own situation. I have to find my brother, no matter what it takes.

Chapter 12

"And the Word was made flesh, and dwelt among us, (and we beheld his glory, the glory as of the only begotten of the Father,) full of grace and truth." - John 1:14 (KJV)

Clueless as I hear cell phones buzzing and ringing. Nurses speak with news of a huge beam that fell into a crowd of the business district. Many were injured and sought medical attention at Miracle.

My mind is racing with all the possibilities of Pat's safety, but there are so few to hold onto. It feels like a cryptic shock wave washing over me, leaving me unsettled and anxious. As I'm lost in my thoughts, I notice a nurse handing a folder labeled "Wellington" to the clerk at the information desk. On the spine of the folder, the number 542 is written.

My heart skips a beat as I gather the courage to ask, "Is that patient available for visitors?" I'm desperately hoping for any reassurance, any small ray of hope that could soften the blows that might come crashing down on me, breaking through my tough exterior and unleashing a flood of pent-up pain that I've held back for years.

Both the clerk and the nurse turn to look at me, their eyes fixed on my trembling form. Unbeknownst to them, their subtle reactions give away the truth. The clerk offers a gentle smile as she places the folder on an open space on her shelf, while the nurse, with a hint of curiosity, asks, "And who might you be?"

"His sister", I murmur.

"Yes, go ahead he was left resting when the aide just left, room 1934," she said calmly.

Joy fills my heart as I scan each number: 1928, 1931, 1934! Each one brings a glimmer of hope, a flicker of possibility. But my bubble of happiness is fragile, like a child's belief in monsters under the bed. I fear that the piercing waves of grief, relentless and cold, will burst my bubble and drown me in sorrow.

In the midst of my anxious footsteps, I notice the nurses locked in a gaze, their eyes transfixed, almost hypnotized. CPR is being performed over my brother's chest, the frantic compressions blending with the rhythm of my racing heart.

"Clear!" a technician calls out, sending a jolt of electricity through his chest. His body jerks in response. The frantic energy fills the air, and an aide rushes back into the room, clutching towels, slamming the door shut in my face. I'm left outside, folded in a mixture of fear and helplessness.

I feel myself falling once again, as if caught in an endless abyss. Where is Seven, the hero of my imagination? I yearn for her presence, for her strength and courage in this moment of uncertainty.

Love Thy Neighbor

Chapter 13

"For we wrestle not against flesh and blood, but against principalities, against powers, against the rulers of the darkness of this world, against spiritual wickedness in high places." - Ephesians 6:12 (KJV)

Religiously, I have loved my family until there was no one left to love.

Let me explain. I am Seven. And things are complicated. Complicated because Joy is not special, and I am not an enigma. You see, I come into existence when the stars align, so to speak. I embody dreams, conquer obstacles, and exude confidence in any situation. I am respectful and never take control without permission. I am, you could say, an equalizer.

As Joy takes a step back, I sense the pent-up rage she has been suppressing for so long. I feel her exhaustion and agony. It's as if a fiery force is slowly creeping up her spine, swelling and surging over her shoulder blades, until the rage spills over into her heart. Emotions hold immense power, they move and never truly dissipate. And I, in turn, absorb all of this, ready to channel her energy outward.

As her ears start to ring and fade into silence, mine become increasingly sharp, attuned to every sound and spiritual vibration. She covers her ears with her hands and lets out a scream, a release of built-up tension. I gather and amplify her strength. The scream reverberates so intensely that it shakes the very foundation of the hospital, as if an earthquake has gripped the entire city. I become electric, throbbing and pulsating, allowing Joy to have a cathartic release. The pitch is so high that it's barely heard by anyone within the building, but nearby dogs and animals run around in circles, trying to make sense of the chaos.

Joy panics and tears stream down her face uncontrollably. She loses strength in her legs and collapses, unconscious. I now preserve her reserves within her, protecting Joy's hidden spaces—her aura, her mind—not to shield her, but to nourish her spirit and bring solace during her rest. I find myself back in solitude, sharpening my sword and preparing to wage war against the notion of peace. The black outs keep happening because Joy hasn't chosen her direction. Joy needs to position her next set of moves to propel herself forward. Joy has to seek out her purpose, gain belief in her abilities and find comfort in knowing that she already belongs.

Chapter 14

"Give alms of thy substance; and when thou givest alms, let not thine eye be envious, neither turn thy face from any poor, and the face of God shall not be turned away from thee." - Tobit 4:7 (KJV Apocrypha)

The hospital surrounds me with an eerie silence, leaving me feeling empty as I descend into a blissful darkness, a realm that only I can perceive. Amidst the darkness, I can faintly hear the scraping of metal against concrete, followed by the sound of footsteps, growing nearer and hastier. Strangely, my limbs remain immobile, unable to respond as Seven approaches and lifts my fragile body. Deeper into the abyss we go, until Seven gently settles my limbs into a deep-seated hammock, cradling me with a sense of security rather than a mere sling. In the distance, a small light begins to shimmer, gradually growing brighter. I notice a tiny flame resting atop Seven's palm.

Raising her gaze, Seven illuminates the arms of my mother, Ocean. Though she doesn't utter a word, her gentle smile speaks volumes as she gazes upward, her focus just beyond her right shoulder. Changing position from kneeling to standing, Seven directs the light towards my father, Jacob.

Bliss washes over me, mingling with waves of regret, love, and guilt. An intense discomfort stirs within my soul, reawakening pains I have never voiced before. How I miss them! They are here, by my side, wait, have they have always been here!

But where are they now? Why have they chosen this moment to reveal themselves? Why did they not come to comfort me sooner? My father catches sight of my face and nods to my mother. In response, she offers a gentle smile, and the unspoken agreement between them flutters through the air like graceful butterflies, reaching my very core. Meeting my father's gaze, he firmly touches my forehead, and in that instant, I sink deep into a memory, guided by his touch.

I was a small, awkward figure with legs like chicken drumsticks and arms as thin as straw, standing at the edge of a silent room filled with other swimmers dressed just as awkwardly. Despite my physical appearance, my presence exuded confidence, strength, and poise. There was no question about my swimming abilities; I simply excelled. It was a God-given talent that had been recognized and praised by others for so long, and I reveled in their admiration. At 13, my focus was on winning, and this time, winning meant securing funding for the community center in my neighborhood.

On the pink and gray brick wall, a white banner hung, its message difficult to decipher but large enough to draw the attention of everyone in the room. The buzzer sounded, and I dove into the water, swimming with all my might to reach the end. I caught glimpses of other girls darting ahead of me, their speed surpassing my own. Determined, I pushed myself harder and harder until I felt myself slipping into a daze.

Suddenly, the scene changed. People rushed to the water's edge as a small smear of blood emerged, mingling with the misty bubbles that refused to settle. A paramedic fought through the frantic parents, their panicked faces as they hurriedly withdrew their daughters from the chaotic water.

My body lay limp as my mother cradled my head, her touch offering both comfort and concern. My father's grip on my hand tightened, his brows furrowing in fear. I had collided with the edge of the pool, my desperation to outpace the others causing me to strike my head. In my pursuit of victory, I had forsaken my own pace.

Amidst the crowd, I spotted my brother, his face etched with fear. Dressed in his favorite basketball jersey, a tribute to the greatest of all time, he looked vulnerable and threatened. I never quite understood the allure of these talented and fearless men who had overcome societal barriers, racism, and personal sacrifices to showcase their God-given abilities.

(Seven) As Joy looks back at herself, I can feel a strong surge of energy. It's like a power awakening inside her, something I've seen before just not in Joy.

Suddenly, Joy wakes up and starts screaming and crying. The whole building shakes from her intense emotions. People panic and rush towards the exit, trying to get away from the chaos.

Amidst the chaos, I see Joy's brother being taken out by their father. They both look scared and uncertain. It's a tense and urgent scene, as if everything is shaking along with Joy's emotions.

Paramedics and Joy's parents try to protect her from falling debris, but it's hard. Her father grabs the banner and uses it as a shield, covering them all.

It's a powerful moment. The banner, once a symbol of achievement, now becomes a shield against danger and a symbol of protection. It shows how far a parent will go to keep their child safe, physically and emotionally.

In that moment, I admire Joy's family for their strength and love. They came together, seeking safety and comfort in each other's presence. It's a reminder of the power of family, even in the face of challenges.

As the world continues to shake around them, I stand by their side, quietly witnessing their struggle. I wonder what lies ahead for Joy and her family, but I know they will face it with resilience and unity. They will find their way through the darkest times, together.

(Joy) The water from the pool overflowed, cascading around me like a torrential downpour. In an instant, everything plunged into darkness once again. The vibrant words on the banner fizzled out, their message fading into obscurity. All that remained were the faint remnants, now barely legible: "Joy's #1 at the Community Pool on Blvd."

As the darkness enveloped me, I felt a surge of conflicting emotions. Pride and accomplishment mingled with a sense of loss and confusion. Being recognized as the number one swimmer at the community pool had been a defining moment in my young life, a testament to my dedication and hard work. But beneath the surface, there was a nagging feeling of emptiness, as if the accolades couldn't fill the void that existed within me.

In that moment, I realized that my pursuit of victory and validation had come at a cost. I had chased external recognition, believing it would bring me lasting happiness and fulfillment. But now, as the darkness closed in, I understood that true meaning and purpose couldn't be found solely in the accolades or the praise of others.

With the fading words on the banner, I let go of the need to prove myself. I recognized the importance of finding my own inner light, one that didn't rely on external validation or the pursuit of perfection. It was a moment of revelation, a turning point in my journey of self-discovery.

In the depths of that darkness, I resolved to seek a different kind of fulfillment, one rooted in authenticity, self-acceptance, and genuine connection. The path ahead might be uncertain, but I was determined to find my own definition of success, one that honored my true self and brought joy beyond the confines of competition.

As the darkness continued to surround me, I embraced the flicker of light within, ready to navigate the unknown and embark on a new chapter of my life.

(Seven) Coming away from the memory, Joy looked at her mother and father and gently fizzled away.

Love Thy Neighbor

Chapter 15

"Cast thy burden upon the LORD, and he shall sustain thee: he shall never suffer the righteous to be moved."
Psalm 55:22, KJV

Nurses surrounded me, checking my blood pressure and tapping my shoulder gently.

"Are you okay?" one of them asked.

"Her heart rate is through the roof!" Another one said.

"Hey we're going to monitor you tonight for safety. Is there anyone you would like to make aware or is your brother your only contact?" She asked sweetly.

I hesitated for a moment, then replied, "Uh, yeah!" it's just my brother." Slumping lower into the hospital chair. Deep down, I knew that my brother was behind a closed hospital door, just like the one I was in. I couldn't help but think about how I had made things worse for both of us, and how everything was going to change once again.

I glanced down and noticed the restraints holding me in place. It was a stark reminder that I couldn't run away anymore, I couldn't fight against what was happening. The constant struggle had left me exhausted and drained.

A heavy sigh escaped my lips as I realized the weight of it all. The realization settled in that I had reached my limit, and I couldn't keep going on like this.

"Hey, why are these here?" Asked upset and confused.

"Oh, you had seizure activity and we needed to keep you from hurting yourself while you were unresponsive." As she faded into a blur as her voice trailed into wisps of whispers.

As I turned my head to the colorless wall the lights slowly dimmed to orange wrapping me in, I thought about Pat and slept.

Love Thy Neighbor

Chapter 16

"Trust in the Lord with all thine heart; and lean not unto thine own understanding. In all thy ways acknowledge him, and he shall direct thy paths."
Proverbs 3:5-6 (KJV)

I sat in the small, sterile room, my heart pounding as I awaited my evaluation with Lauren, the intake nurse at Miracle Memorial Hospital. The air felt heavy with tension, and I couldn't help but fidget with anticipation. I wondered what questions she would ask and how I would answer them. This morning all sorts of people came buzzing in and out of my room. I got an I.V. some how in the middle of the night. I ate what little I could of breakfast before Dr. What's his name came in shook his head a couple times to another Dr. and they both walked back out leaving my nurse whose name is Lauren. Lauren said she'd be back to ask me some questions after checking on everyone else. Well happy 1st day of being 17.

When Lauren walked out I finished the rest of my juice and had to go to the bathroom. I couldn't move to go because of these stupid bracelets. I called for help using the buzzer and a nurse aide came in to help me. She watched me like those guards watch prisoners in jail. I used to watch clips of "Scared Straight" and I felt like it was happening to me. When I finished she helped me back in bed and put the bracelets back on-tight.

Then, Lauren entered the room with a warm smile that immediately put me at ease. She carried a clipboard filled with papers, with sunflower stickers on top, ready to dig deep into my history and experiences. "Hey, Joy. How are you doing today?" she asked, her voice filled with genuine care. I think some people underestimate how their voice plays apart in comforting someone else because I immediately felt like things were going to be okay.

I looked up, my nerves evident in my trembling voice. "I... I'm feeling a bit overwhelmed," I confessed. "I'm scared about what comes next, about what's about to happen to me here."

Lauren nodded empathetically; her eyes filled with understanding. "It's completely normal to feel that way, Joy. This is a new journey for you, and it can be intimidating. But I want you to know that we're here to support you every step of the way. We want to help you heal and find peace."

As Lauren began asking questions, her tone gentle and non-judgmental, I opened up about my experiences. I shared the pain and struggles that had shaped my life, the heavy burden I had carried for so long. It felt both relieving and painful to finally let it all out, to be honest about the wounds that ran deep. Throughout our conversation, Lauren listened attentively, offering words of comfort when needed. She made me feel safe, allowing me to open

Love Thy Neighbor

up about my grief, anxiety, and depression. It was as if she could see the turmoil inside me and genuinely wanted to help.

As our discussion neared its end, Lauren noticed the visible discomfort on my face as I tried to rub each one of my wrists, the marks from the restraints were welts.. She saw the lingering effects of the restraints and sensed that I needed them to be released and that I could be trusted not to harm myself.

"Joy, I can see that you're feeling much calmer now," Lauren observed, her voice filled with compassion. "I believe it's important for you to have a little physical freedom at this moment. You've shown great strength and cooperation throughout our conversation."

With a gentle smile, Lauren made the decision to release me from the restraints, allowing me to experience a newfound sense of freedom within the evaluation room. It was a small gesture, but it meant the world to me. As she unlocked the restraints, I felt a weight lift off my shoulders, both literally and metaphorically.

I took a moment to process the significance of this act. The chaffing on my wrists served as a reminder of the struggles I had endured, but it also symbolized my resilience. I gently rubbed my wrists, embracing the physical release and the freedom it represented.

Looking at me with empathy, Lauren acknowledged the significance of this moment. "Remember, Joy, you are more than the restraints that once confined you. You are strong, and we are here to guide you towards healing and freedom."

I nodded, a sense of gratitude washing over me. I appreciated Lauren's understanding and support. In that moment, I allowed myself to believe that I could break free from the chains of my past and create a brighter future. Even though I couldn't tell her everything in such a short period of time. Before leaving Lauren stood up grabbing her clipboard and all her paperwork, placing the heap underneath her left arm and she uttered words that confused me.

"Joy, tomorrow you will be transferred."

Transferred? I replied.

"Yes, to what we call the psychiatric wing. I have full confidence that you will be fine and well taken care of. This wing we're on now only helps heal physically wounds. Where you're going you'll be able to heal mentally. Okay?"

    I tried to force out my frustration, anger, and confusion into weaponized words, but "okay" was the only one that slipped through my lips. A solemn word that made me feel defeated and lonely in my mind.

With my wrists no longer bound, I held onto the newfound sense of freedom, both physically and emotionally. I knew that my journey towards healing was far from over, but in this moment, I cherished the small victory. The welts became itchy with the chaffing from the padding on the restraint cuffs. Resting my focus on my wrists they had become a symbol of my strength and resilience, a reminder that I had the power to overcome the challenges that lay ahead. I held onto the belief that I could take back my life from the shadows of my past. The welts would heal into scars on my wrists and serve as a constant reminder of the strength I had to discover within myself. With the support of people like Lauren, I was determined to embrace the freedom I deserved and build a brighter future for myself no matter what.

Love Thy Neighbor

Chapter 17

"Be strong and of a good courage, fear not, nor be afraid of them: for the Lord thy God, he it is that doth go with thee; he will not fail thee, nor forsake thee." - Deuteronomy 31:6 (KJV)

After a week in the psych ward waiting on answers I began to feel numb. I started hearing sounds like they were distant and not as close as the hallway that was adjacent to my room door.

Nelly is my roommate and for all I know she's a saint. She sits on her bed rocking, almost all day, if they didn't come force feed her medications at the same time every day and make her go to the restroom I don't think she would ever leave her bed.

Don't ask me what time it is either because these slimy guards have taken every clock off every wall and wrist in here. The only time I've ever noticed was when a guard's cell phone alarm rang by mistake. It was a rooster and it said "nooooon time" real loud. It echoed into every chamber in this place. I bet it even alerted people in the saddest crevices.

By lunch I was sitting at an aluminum table sketching an imaginary drawing of Seven, wishing she would take on life. My life today is another day in a hole. I mean in this place it's actually not bad just everything is all white and everything that is not white is gray and anything that's not gray it's black and those black lines remind me of sketching; they remind me of drawing they remind me of my past life. I know that it wasn't that long ago. What's so hypnotizing is the way everybody moves around here, it is like nothing ever changes, the routines are disciplined and enforced to a "T".

All of a sudden I hear a large door slam shut. I've never heard that in here. I get up off the metal chair and look out the door left then right. I don't see anyone and I don't hear anything.

Immediately I started to hear scuffling feet moving across the shiny slippery white floor, in their laborious heavy shadows. You, come here!

I think to myself they cannot be pointing at me. I look to the left again to make sure there wasn't anyone else in the hallway. Pulling my head back inside the door I quickly sit back down at the table and after a few moments one of them grabbed me.

Ow! I yelled.

"It's time to go to your room."The guard said sternly.

He gripped my shoulder tightly and forcefully pushed me into Nelly inside our room where another guard was waiting.. By the time I stumbled to my bed, I looked up after catching my balance to look at him. He just stood right here, waiting at the head of Nelly's bed. The other guard yelled, "sit down now!" He began grabbing me from the back of my standard issued white t-shirt almost tearing the seem. "I hate this place!" I scream. I don't even know where they came from or why they're doing this to me. I look over at Nelly swaying carelessly until she closes her eyes and stops.

Afraid I focus on my freedom, I grab the forearm of the guard grabbing me with my left hand and I begin to twist his arm to the inside of his chest. I punched the top of his forehead. The guard's hair swung back to the other guy as he was grabbing me, I kick him with my left leg in his torso. I kick him so hard, I kick him so tough that when I kick him once more, he buckles into the wall and doesn't get up. The warden, the beast of this place yells "grab her!" I grabbed the next guard with a bear hug and squeeze his ribs. He screams out a sigh that I haven't heard from anyone ever before. *What is happening to me?*

Chapter 18

"Ye shall not fear them: for the LORD your God he shall fight for you." - Deuteronomy 3:22 (KJV)

I yelled out a warrior cry and braced myself to get on top of the one on the left. I jumped on him and started biting him like a dog, hard and unforgiving. He started cursing.

"GET HER OFF ME," he yelped.

"Naw man I'm out" and the other one started running out.

And there she appears, the beast, the warden, the Sergeant, Director Cowell.

She turns and look at me as if she wasn't scared. I look over at Nelly as she has begun to rock gently once again. I said to the Director in a very low tone almost a growl "if you *were* the boss you would've had patience, but because you did not have patience you will never be the boss, the next time you see me I will end you." Her face cracks for a sliver of an instant, yet enough to focus on my last words as if they were concrete stones falling from above a cliff as she stood underneath. "…because you did not have the patience for all of us." I sternly finish.

"Is that a threat?" She asked creepily.

"Of course, Director Cow-ell, it's your prophecy," I say. With the realization that I could control that fate a genuine smirk paints itself across my face. Her countenance and outward appearance though professional is lifeless. She takes her fingers aiming at me like a gun and says "you draw first, little lady." I didn't take both of mine and point back at hers. I want her to know that even if I forget all about her that I never will. I see her all the way down to her core, the nasty filthiness of people who feel like they are in control of other people for money or power. I've never felt this adrenaline this way and it overpowered me; however, mine is such a divine feeling that I've never felt before.

The warden's secure stance breaks as she squirms away taking what must have felt uncomfortable and forming that into each calculated step backwards, exiting and quickly locking the door, then jogging in a cadence only Beethoven would appreciate because each sound of the click of her heels are so pronounced and heavy, then light and echoing almost fading into no existence and then reemerging again against those thick concrete walls in the hallway. Her fear is obvious and music to my ears.

I hear a heavier door slam this time and I run to the window inside of the white cell. *It's Pat!*

Chapter 19

"But the fruit of the spirit is love, joy, peace, long suffering, gentleness, goodness, faith, meekness, temperance: against such there is no law." - Galatians 5:22-23 (KJV)

That sound was the sound of his door closing. I ran towards the sound. Allowing my ears to guide me. My brother was alive. A tear rolled down my face. I could not stay here another night after what just happened, I had to go. The adrenaline ran right out of my system like a bathtub releasing its water down the drain.

I have no clue where that even came from. I wish that I had my notebook, I wish I could write, I wish that I could draw or sit in my bed and draw. That's what I need to do. maybe I can pull a piece of the paint off with my fingernail and draw piece of her I just need to talk to Seven. I need her to stand up for me! I need

Seven to do what I need to happen here, to get me out of here. I just don't know how to do it. I start welling up, tears simple tears race slowly down each one of my cheeks. After fighting so strongly, I am now retracting. I am now me.

Reflecting, I think about it for a second, maybe that was Seven! Just like at the hospital when the beam fell in the business district. I know that some how my energy creates in my world when I sketch in the imaginary world.

I can't let my brother leave without me what should I do?

I can feel my palms tingling. I look at my roommate she's looking at me. I've never seen Nelly look at anything or anyone in particular, not a light switch, not the floor, nothing she just sits there and rocks all day. Nelly's long black hair swinging gently with her caramel brown skin uncreased is pretty much what I see when I get up and lay down. Now, I can finally see her eyes and they are the color of the rainbow. That is why they look black from afar. I've never seen anything so extraordinary. She says "finally…you've walked into you, now don't second guess your strength, ignite."

Chapter 20

"Now thanks be unto God, which always causeth us to triumph in Christ, and maketh manifest the savour of his knowledge by us in every place." - 2 Corinthians 2:14 (KJV)

Following that feeling, that pride I felt with Seven. I pulled the entire screen off the window. I kept kicking it like I kicked the guard over and over and over again. I heard my knee crack but I kept kicking and kept kicking almost as if I was in the backseat of my mind and the inner me stepped up, it worked! The window fell out freely. While watching the window fall I heard the door slam and lock but it didn't matter I was getting out of here! I turned back to look at Nelly and said goodbye, but she was gone.

As my brother's truck began to back out and pull away I realized that all I could do was jump. I looked all the way down and even though I was in the backseat of my mind and afraid Seven jumped!

We fell into the bushes, or she fell into the bushes or I fell into the bushes, but either way we're out of here. I reset my knee back into place and began running as fast as I could. Running as fast as I used to swim at the community center. I ran so fast I could feel the wind rushing past my cheeks. I can feel my hair bouncing up and down. I could feel my back. I could feel all of my muscles. I could feel myself growing in areas that I've never grown before. My feet were barely touching the concrete with these cracked shoes, they were slipping across the pavement and I still had to catch up.

I'm trying to pace myself harder to catch up to Pat. Why can't he see me? Why is he not looking out his rearview mirror? I cannot believe that he is alive, and I have to catch him. I am going to catch him. He's the only one left, he's the only one left in our family that knows me.

As I'm running, I realize that Seven will support me. Yell Seven! I need to scream, I need to scream so Pat knows that it's me. I need to scream while I'm running so Pat will stop and if Pat will not stop on his own, I will stop him with my scream. I began to scream out "Patrick Kareem, Pat it's me!" Stop! Stop now! I begin to elevate my voice even louder. Pat, stop now! The truck started to slow down. He looked in his rearview mirror and completely stopped the truck.

My emotions overwhelmed me, and I begin to say Pat's name so loud that it broke the street apart, splitting several deep cracks into the road.

Thank goodness it was such a small crack by the tire that it could fit in the space of the crack but not devour a fourth of the truck.

With my emotions way past my body and deeply dialing into some visceral "outer space" my spirit felt foolish that this was happening again. I was detained, transported, contained and escaped violently for what? Releasing my emotions. Why is yelling deemed dangerous? Wait, can the police send me back to the Director? Will yelling like I did in the hospital alert people that could send me away for good? I mean they have physical proof now because of the road. Can this power really be deemed dangerous?

As he jumped out in disbelief I ran into my brother, and I couldn't let him go. I started to cry. Even though Pat has been so mean to me the past few years since our parents died he was all I had and I was relieved.

Love Thy Neighbor

Chapter 21

"And bring hither the fatted calf, and kill it; and let us eat, and be merry: For this my son was dead, and is alive again; he was lost, and is found. And they began to be merry." - Luke 15:23-24 (KJV)

P at swung his car door open and was about to jump in, but then he looked back at me with surprise.

"Joy, they told me that you couldn't leave," he said, his voice sounding both excited and worried.

"What!" I shouted.

"I'm really sorry things turned out like this. They said you had to stay for a while." He walked over to me and gently shook my shoulders, like he was scared almost like I might could disappear.

"Can you believe it?" Pat's voice sounded like he couldn't believe his eyes. "It's been a whole six months since I saw you last."

My heart started racing. "Six months!"

I couldn't wrap my head around it. Believing I'd only been away for a week, maybe two, when I searched my mind for a timeline my head suddenly hurt, and I squinted, feeling like I might throw up.

"Yes, Joy, six months," Pat repeated, looking even more confused.

"Come on, hop in," he said quickly.

I rushed to the other side of the car, holding the left side of my head and opening the door with my right hand. I slid into the seat and memories of the last time I rode in his car flashed in my mind. Even though a lot of time had gone by, my body still felt scared. I looked around, remembering Pat grabbing my coat, and I tried to remember the past six months in that place. It was all blurry, but I could remember Nelly."The place I was in made everything feel strange and blurry," my head still feeling muddled.

"Hey, the hospital released your phone and backpack to me when I was released. I looked at your sketches – I couldn't believe it, Joy…you have the power."

Love Thy Neighbor

Chapter 22

"For our gospel came not unto you in word only, but also in power, and in the Holy Ghost, and in much assurance; as ye know what manner of men we were among you for your sake." - 1 Thessalonians 1:5 (KJV)

Pat handed me his phone, showing me news articles about good things happening in the city.

"Look, Joy," he said, pointing at the screen. "See, things are changing out here." He looked really hopeful and saved the top three articles.

The first article interviewed homeless families getting approved for housing inside apartments. A new foundation emerged in the city granting funds to establish housing for families to become stable allowing them to become apart of society again.

The second article told the uplifting story of helping workers who lost their jobs, giving them homes and money to help them become stabile. This included an addition to the employment office with appointed staff that could train individuals on beneficial skills for employment. They were held accountable by practicing communication skills, role playing 20 hours of interpersonal skills and so much more. Once they completed several of the skills they received grants to complete a certificate program and $200 for clothing that matched the profession they completed.

The third article was about high school juniors and seniors getting to learn from professionals in different jobs, like plumbing and electricity. Passion was in one of the pictures, and she looked really happy.

I felt giddy. My heart was challenged with gratitude.in this moment the light just pushed past the darkness that felt crusted to my view of the world. Seeing each article, freedom, Pat with me and not in the hospital gave energy to that hope I found in the hospital after talking to Lauren.

"I'm so glad you're here," I told him, and I felt a bit lighter. But then I got confused again. "Wait, Pat, what's the power and what is 'it' being used for?" I asked him.

Smiling Pat explained, "We'll get there Joy. I'm just happy that the special power is being used to help people."

I looked out the window and felt the wind on my face. "How do you know?" I asked.

Everything felt unsure, but having Pat next to me made me feel better. The road ahead might be a mystery, but with Pat by my side, I felt like I could handle whatever was coming.

"There's just so much to unravel, Pat." I said quietly.

"I know "he said.

Chapter 23

"The lips of the wise disperse knowledge: but the heart of the foolish doeth not so" - Proverbs 15:7 (KJV)

Hearing sirens, I melted into the same seat that I sat in after having the fight on the bus; with Pat screaming at me right before Vena hit him in the head. Pat could have left me in the psychiatric ward alone. Remembering how much it seemed he had been hating my guts.

Confused I asked "Pat, why were you there today?"

"Since being released from the hospital I've been coming every Thursday."

"Oh, for real?" I piped.

"It took me a little bit to track you down. You know after getting your things from the hospital I was confused. I called over to Vena's and really could get very far with her. So, I called our older sister."

"What!"

"Yeah, long story, not for today though."

I nodded slowly.

"Well I got the word through text where you were and started checking on you to see how things were going. The Director would say that you never wanted to see me and that seeing me would make things even worse, but I knew better.

"How did you know better?" I asked him.

"When we were younger doctors would call or come by interested in you, wanting to take you in for tests. Mom and Dad would angrily disagree because they had old brain scans from when you were very young."

"Why Pat, what was wrong with me?" I shot back.

"Wait, let me finish telling you about this first and then I'll tell you more about that Joy," he said calmly.

"Ok." I replied.

"The Director would push and say things like migraines, expressive episodes or whatever else "worse" could mean. She gave me those excuses to keep me from pushing too hard. Last Thursday day the Director told me that losing you was the best thing that could have happened to me. I walked away disagreeing just like I remember Mom and Dad doing."

"She really said that?" I asked panicked.

"Yeah, she did."He said in a faint whisper.

"Wow." I said flatly.

"Finally, freedom seemed way more boring than I care to say. Hearing my truth and not the Director's fantasies gave me the direction I needed, Joy, it cleared my head. I left today knowing I was going to call the news to bring attention to the facility until I got you back. You're not ready to be thrown to the world and asked to conquer it, Joy, and in my opinion there's too many people asked to do that before they're ready." Pat clinched he jaw and silently drove for a few minutes.

I sat in silence with him just speechless.

"Listen Joy the truth is what happened at the swimming community center wasn't taboo. You have some old energy from dad's side of our family. Energy that's so unconscionable that it draws force from the stars."

"The stars!" I yelled.

"Yes, and because of that episode I've been fighting federal agents for years, Joy, they think you're some alien freak or something. I had been trying to stop them from taking you and scientifically dissecting every inch of your body to find the catalyst to your power, but dad already gave me answers a long time ago." Pat weaves a trail of incoherent sentences, I hear one here then another there. I can't hold anymore, with the sirens lagging behind, I fade.

Love Thy Neighbor

Chapter 24

"Cast thy burden upon the Lord, and he shall sustain thee: he shall never suffer the righteous to be moved." - Psalm 55:22

(KJV)

Pat has had such a hard time holding onto both of us for so long and I never even knew it. All the changes, the mood swings, the fights. I used to think that he was going crazy with me. Now that I've been in that facility, I realize that being crazy doesn't mean you're crazy. Sometimes being unique or being different makes the world think you're crazy. When the world thinks you're crazy it will challenge you and then cast you out.

Pat looks at me and snaps the truck miles down the road as I sit up. He doesn't care about what's about to happen.

"Hey where's the sirens?" I ask.

He laughed "Joy that was yesterday."

"Yesterday," I yawn.

"Joy I need to at least tell you that the power you have inside is the push and drive that has always stopped any adversity. It has to be nurtured and protected. I'm going to find a safe space to help you tap into our ancestors, ok?"

"Um okay," I awkwardly reply.

"I was a star athlete because our family raised me to be your protection until you became strong enough to protect yourself – you know, to be all competitive and strong was meant to grow me up mentally and physically. However, I had a job to do, Joy, dad would tell me that one day I would have to be a hero. The day at the swim competition I thought that was my chance to to be that hero, but dad shut me out. I thought dad thought I wasn't capable. I thought all these years that you sabotaged my moment to prove to him and mom that I could do it. I'm sorry Joy, for being so stupid before, I was just sad."

"Seriously, Pat, wow, I've always admired your strength and that competitive fire in you, to me you've always been a superhero even if it was in a villain's costume for a little while.Thank you for telling me... you'll always be my big brother. Thanks again for looking out for me even now."

"Joy, our ancestors followed this pattern too – older brother then little sister. And these sisters, like you, had the same "Hilda energy" thing going on."

I laughed, "Hilda energy"? What's that even mean?

"It's like this mega-strong vibe when channeled correctly can change physical reality. Over time, it got all sneaky and settled into our minds. Like a secret power guiding us, connecting us to the past."

"Wait, so this energy has been passed down all the way to us?"

"Bingo! Our family stories have kept this energy alive. It's like this super old-school legacy we're in."

"See Pat! You're not just my big brother. You're like the guardian of our family's power, without you I would know nothing and to be honest I still feel like I only get the tip of the ice berg."

"And you, Joy, you're the one who keeps the legacy alive. We're a team, carrying the family story and this energy thing that makes us who we are. Don't worry I'm getting ready to pull over."

I nodded to Pat in silence. I was not passed the information from my father because of the accident. Pat knew large pieces because he was older and was able to consume the stories in bits and pieces as he grew, before our family was killed by my unstable power.

Love Thy Neighbor

Chapter 25

"The Lord is my strength and my shield; my heart trusted in him, and I am helped: therefore my heart greatly rejoiceth; and with my song will I praise him." - Psalm 28:7 (KJV)

I began struggling in my seat.

"Pat what am I supposed to do? I mean it's not like there's an instruction manual." I roared.

"Yeah, ugh, I don't really know how you do it. I mean how do you help all those people like on the articles I just showed you, or how did you make all that water flood the center?" He said piped back.

As I thought about it this is the first day I realized that I could control the energy through my emotions. "Pat, it's my emotions, every time I feel overwhelmed or scared, it's my feelings!" I stuttered.

"Yeah, but the emotion is not stable. Joy, how did you crack the road yesterday?" He asked softly.

Excited I have a flood of memories proving that I move things with my emotions when I focus on an image or thought.

"It's my memories. My thoughts…well, my pictures that I can hold in my minds eye view." I said softly.

"Ok, ok, now we're getting somewhere!" He replied enthusiastically.

Pat didn't stop the truck because he wanted to honestly see if I could harness the power of what I call Seven now I know they called this Hilda. I have been bottling my most powerful self up internally. Drawing Seven really gave me an outlet to release the energy safely ~ sort of because it really did change things in my world.

"You know Joy that the energy is complete all by itself?"

"Pat, I call Hilda energy Seven. So, is Seven complete?" Sounding unsure . "Yes, Seven has always been complete. When the energy is displaced or suppressed there are others that will emerge and balance Seven's energy allowing you to surface and become one."

Tilting my head I told Pat my memory had this patches in them. Pat reassured me that I would be fine, just relax into the energy and fully be Joy. He couldn't officially tell me anything before confirmation that it wasn't just me out of anger but out of love.

"Wait, Nelly! I exclaimed.

"Nelly?" Pat questioned.

"Yes, Nelly, she wasn't real, with flesh and bone Pat! Thank you, thank you, thank you!" I said fully of Joy.

Cracking the street pressured those anxieties inside me proving to Pat that I finally won over my tangled emotions. I felt my veins growing, I felt my heart beating, I felt my breath.

"Remember Mom & Dad's cure for chaos, Joy?"

"Yes, I do." Replying frankly.

Calming my mind enough to begin meditation I search for the perfect image yet choose my life's mantra. Pat continues to park the the car backwards in a end spot looking over a host of trees. The parking lot is covered with two levels beneath us a three above us it's halfway full with no other people in sight.

I can feel the humming of the engine throughout my body. I focused on my frail mess, my brokenness, and all the misinformation I consumed in various ways that created invisible stressors. I held on to those. Releasing them one by one allowing me to fall into a deep space. The space I exist in when I sketch. The fog of not knowing how things will end is only the feeling between the strokes of my pencil to my pad. I am free to create in an open space- my mind. I am nervous. My hands are sweating. Pat looks over at me before I close my eyes and says, "you don't have to worry about security just fall."

Love Thy Neighbor

Chapter 26

"For God hath not given us the spirit of fear; but of power, and of love, and of a sound mind." - 2 Timothy 1:7 (KJV)

Darkness turns slowly into light and I see a pond with full trees surrounding the water locking in the space like security. I see Seven and her sword cemented in the dirt. I read the words going down again to remind myself - Love yourself Joy, love yourself as others have loved you, Love yourself as you Love your neighbor. Seven is wearing all black as she usually does; however, this time, she doesn't have any of the armor that she usually wears; it's almost like it's linen flowing in the air. Her hair is released from her head cover. Relaxed she takes her mask gently off her face and it hits the ground. Seven is directly across the pond. The linen is deep purple with gold accents as a gentle light rises and she creeps closer. She begins to walk into the water, so I begin to walk slowly into the water. I have so many questions for her, but I can feel so much distance as she is so far away from me. I begin to walk closer and closer until my foot gently lowers into the warm base of the dark pond. Honestly, there's no bottom to this pond. It's only water but I'm walking. The water is up to my belly button, and I continue to walk without feeling any solid dirt to trust my steps on. We continue to walk, and I continue to think Seven is looking right past me with her gaze; however, her eyes are piercing into mine. As we almost get to the middle Seven takes both of her hands and puts them together, palms up. She reaches out for me but not for me to grab her hands. But for me to realize that she is giving something to me. As I stare deeper there is nothing in her hands. Gliding forward I'm almost close enough to see the bottom of her palms.

Now, I see for sure there is nothing there. I put my hand over my heart, then dug it inside of my chest. I did not break any skin the way I thought it would. I can feel myself losing feeling. A small pool of blood rushes into the palm of my hand. I can hear Pat saying, "Joy be free."

I see the trees swaying so I know that that is the security of my brother around this pond.

I realize as I'm digging into the innermost parts of my chest that the reason why there is no response from me as I am going through all these daily struggles is because I have no connections to my past.

As I take my dark beating heart out slowly, I can still feel life coursing through my veins. My body is still pulsating..

I put my heart inside of Seven's palms; my heart now is making its way inside of her black kimono inside of her chest.

By pulling down the black garment Seven shows me that the heart inside of her chest was a match. I was consumed in gratitude. Mine became a shadow on top of hers and both hearts merged red, thriving, and living. I am Seven.

Love Thy Neighbor

Chapter 27

"And I knew that thou hearest me always: but because of the people which stand by I said it, that they may believe that thou hast sent me. And when he thus had spoken, he cried with a loud voice, Lazarus, come forth. And he that was dead came forth, bound hand and foot with graveclothes: and his face was bound about with a napkin. Jesus saith unto them, Loose him, and let him go." - John 11:39-44 (KJV)

My body drops into the pond like the bottom just released and we fall. We fall beneath the water now where my feet were not touching. I became conscious of this undefined vast space, sort of like the time when Seven brought me to my parents. Am I in space? It feels like I'm being watched but I see nothing only darkness with specs of silver glitter everywhere.

Love Thy Neighbor

I looked around and I saw a room full of people; family and people with another family as I turned around more floating gently. I did not need air to sustain myself.

I could feel all their emotions and feelings. I just needed to connect. Seven pulls me because I can see through the water into the pond as it is no longer dark and murky.

The world is no longer around us with safety and security. The trees- Pat were thinning out, no longer were the tops as thick as maple trees. I look back at the families, and they had become one. Blending in with one another, but you could pick them out from amongst one another by their clothes, jewelry and swagger. I look at Seven and she bows. That is when I feel my ancestors pulling at me by my feet. *Am I dying?*

Chapter 28

"And they were all filled with the Holy Ghost, and began to speak with other tongues, as the Spirit gave them utterance." - Acts 2:4

Does this mean they know me? *I mean could they?* Looking around everyone seemed interested in me. Seven pulls my hand towards her. I move gently into her space and Seven merged over me and I feel complete.

They're talking to me!

Inside of my mind now I can hear.

I am receiving an abundance of warm love, of praise for making it here. I ask what is here? They respond "home".

They are so proud of our family even with all the adversity- and fighting - just as they have fought through time.

I ask why my parents weren't "home"?

With one coherent pressing of my heart, I felt and heard this collective message: that they are still being held onto through me. Release them and they will come, leave the guilt, leave the sadness for not remembering, relinquish the burden of protection, let go of the passion you surround yourself with that locks in the hatred. Surrender your what ifs and let be.

Love Thy Neighbor

Chapter 29

"And he took bread, and gave thanks, and break it, and gave unto them, saying, This is my body which is given for you: this do in remembrance of me." - Luke 22:19

I know that this is Seven pulling into control because the energy is intensive and full of certainty. I trust all of me and then the language begins to make sense. The atmosphere begins to change, and I feel like it is not a safe space anymore.

I know it's all of you.

Please, I want to come out of this meditation or deep sleep or whatever and remember. I mean I can write all of this down but how? I want to sketch every single one of their faces in my notepad. I want to contain their presence.

I want to mark this space. I begin to cry, and scream and cry.

Love Thy Neighbor

I feel as if I can only soak in all of myself. It seems like there are hundreds of people crowding me.

How can I be a part of a family so large and not one person stands out? How can everyone be so mesmerizing.

And that is when She walks closer to me.

Chapter 30

"The king's daughter is all glorious within: her clothing is of wrought gold." - Psalm 45:13

She's divine, she's beautiful and she touches my heart. The atmosphere releases me again and I fall through a black hole.

I open my eyes in the car with Pat. With the truck seat leaned back as far as it would go.

Pat looks at me.

He was right, we were safe and now it's time to move on but where do we move onto?

Me, Pat and Seven.

So now say it with me: "I will Love myself, I will Love myself as others have given freely to me, I will Love myself, to be able to give Love freely to my neighbor."

Forgive.

Release.

Conquer.

Receive.

Sans Souci

Do not forget…

The Director must go.

Love Thy Neighbor

"For all the law is fulfilled in one word, even in this; Thou shalt love thy neighbour as thyself."

Galatians 5:14 (KJV)